Mona's Masterpiece
[ˈmastərˌpēs]
Fifty Pieces of Poetry

By: Monica Alfred

Written by: Monica Alfred
Copyright © 2018

Website: www.monasmasterpiece.com
Email:monamasterpiece@yahoo.com
ISBN-13:
978-0692737200

ISBN-10:
0692737200

ALL RIGHTS RESERVED
All rights reserved in all media. No part of this book may be used or reproduced in any manner whatsoever without written permission, except in the case of brief quotations embodied in critical articles and reviews.

Masterpiece
A work of outstanding artistry, skill, or workmanship:
"A great literary masterpiece."

I am still learning how to put it all together, All of the pieces you left broken are put into these poems.
-Monica

-Dedication:

This book was written with the purpose of leaving a legacy behind. For so long, I sought my purpose not realizing that my purpose was to uplift others by being naked with vulnerability while expressing the darkest and happiest moments in my life. In this book, I give a piece of my heart to the world.

To my Daughter Keymoni, when I felt like nothing you made me feel like everything. Thank you for being the light of my life. You encourage me to keep going when all I wanted to do is stop. I want you to be all that I could not be and more.

Keep thriving, keep shining, like the star you are bound to be.

To my son Keith, in a society where it is set up for you to lose; I want you win. I need you to be the man that God destined you to be. Be a provider, a protector, and a foundation.

To my daddy John, thank you for always listening when no one else could hear my cries.

You can rest assured that I have finally found my voice.

To my mother Monique, you are and forever will be my Queen in spirit and in presence and if I have never told you before; Thank you for all that you do.

To my brothers, Jerry you are the glue of our family, and despite how chaotic you can be at times, you are our peace.

I love and look up to you.

To James my big brother, I love you unconditionally.

To Kenny, Herbert, and all known and unknown you will forever be in my heart.

To the men that gave me pain and heartache I wish you bliss...through my sorrow which I thought would be the death of me you gave me life. You gave me the strength to write my hurt. I survived you.

To the L.O.M.L

I have always been able to express my words on paper but I find it difficult to put into words all that I honor and admire about you; in spite of that, it is essential for you to know that I have more respect, trust and adoration for you than anyone else in the world.
Life has dealt you a difficult hand, but your drive, determinism, and dedication to play the cards you've been dealt is to be honored.
You put your all into what you aim to achieve and for that, I admire you.
I commend you for your loyalty and humility, In addition to all of the love, fascination and joy you give me; you have also provided me with security, comfort and protection in my most tender moments. Through disappointments, pain and depression you have always been by my side.

You have mourned my losses and my heartache as if they were your own.
Even in the times when we would tear each other down, you never gave up on me, we never abandoned each other,
and for that, I am eternally grateful.
I am grateful for all of you, all of the pieces of you that you have kept sacred and left for only me to see, and all the support you have bestowed upon me.
You are the most genuine love I have ever felt and even though I may make it hard to love me, you love me anyway.
You are the ultimate compliment, the optimum balance, the exact key to my equilibrium, the picture perfect piece to my puzzle.

Thank you for giving me the encouragement to keep writing, thank you for your patience and understanding, thank you for your time and your love, thank you for not just loving me with your words but with your actions. When my heart seemed to be empty, you filled me up with so much joy and peace. You are a dream come true when I felt like I was living a nightmare. You are my heaven on earth and I am forever grateful for your presence and the impact you have in my life.
You are and will forever be

My first, my choice, my headache, my Jaco.

To my Lord and Savior, Thank you for giving me a love that is sufficient, faithful, forgiving and everlasting. When I was broken, you nurse me back to health, you restored me, replenished my spirit and you renewed my heart.

Contents:

Intro Poem: Purpose

Unravel

The Rose That Grew From Concrete

Mother

My Child

Son

Overnight

S.W.A.K

Prey

Abortion

Garden

Cactus

Once Upon a Time

Half

Intoxicated

Drowning

Catch

Sugar

Walls

Insomniac

Performance

Pretend

Carpenter

Bag Man

Slave

Vows

Curse

Hungry

Conflict

Robbery

Band-Aid

Death

Senses

Recipe to recovery

Karma

RX

Bending Blues

Incompetence

Acceptance

Reborn

Naked

Woman

Homemade

Sweet Tea

Custom-made

Artist

Live

Mona Lisa

Ayiti (Haiti)

Ayiti (Creole Version)

Survival

Poetry

Bonus Poem: Resilience

Purpose

For the voiceless
With eyes that scream for help,

For the young ones
with swallowed tongues
and lips stitched in fear,

For the broken
 whose shattered hearts
are destroyed into tiny pieces,

For the caged girl
who wishes to sing,

For the numb
who prays to feel,

For the lost
who seek freedom and truth,

For the scorned who craves
healing from hurt,

This
 Book
 Is
For
You…

Unravel

Open my book and read me,

Come into my world and feel

Everything

I feel for you.

Use your mind to visualize my words and see through me.

Transparency at its finest.

Use your hands to feel

The print of my letters

Your fingers to flip through my pages.

Touch me.

Feel my vulnerability and

Discover parts of me that doesn't even exist

Yet.

Caress my book

And hold on to it dearly

Get into it deeply.

Inhale it.

Soak in my scent.

Learn all of me.

Let my poetry consume you

Allow my words to flow sweetly from your mouth

And savor my nakedness.

Listen to my words

Hear them.

Understand them.

Read my soul…. READ ME.

The rose that grew from concrete

(Homage to Tupac Amaru Shakur)

The rose that grew from concrete proved that nature's law was wrong.

It flowered despite its circumstance and produced where it did not belong.

Undeterred by its adversity in being planted in stone

It arose where other flowers had never ever grown.

It slipped between the cracks

with its will to breathe fresh air.

It sprouted from its soil

and flourished without a care.

It thrived without its sources,

deprived of water and the sun.

It ached for spring through all its barriers

It dreams remain undone.

Complete with damage petals, its thorns and pain unspoken.

Just like the rose that grew from concrete

I AM the woman that *bloomed* from *broken*.

Mother

Your entire existence

is centered on being great.

Working hard to

develop my future

I have watched you get knocked down and

Find your way back up.

Defying all odds,

Set before you.

Your strength is like a tree

deeply rooted into the earth's surface.

You've taught me how to survive through suffering

You've taught me how to look

at life's struggles in the eye and fight back

You hid tears behind smiles and moved despite the weight you carried.

I try to emulate your actions

Hoping to be half the woman you are

But you want me to be better.

You are scarred yet strong and sanctified

You taught me how to be unbreakable.

You taught me how to be a

Powerful

Black

Woman.

But most importantly

You taught me that

Crowns may tilt.

But only Queens

 Adjust them.

My Child

Pregnant with possibility

Yet full of uncertainty.

A big 'ol belly of what if's.

Scared of how everyone would judge me.

Another statistic.

A child having a baby.

Afraid of how my small frame would endure you.

But you were already planted,

Conceived with love,

and destined for greatness.

My complex child.

You are my light within my darkness

My teacher and my student

My sun and my star

My truest and purest form.

My gem.

Always smiling.

Always learning.

Always loving and childlike.

From belly to sitting Indian style

Between my legs

While I part & grease your scalp

and decorate your hair with barrettes and ribbons.

You are my everything.

And if anything should happen to me

People would be able to see

a glimpse of me through you.

My child,

I love everything about your admirable spirit.

The way you nurture your imagination,

Embrace the universe,

and express your creativity.

My child you are captivating.

My child,

   I

Simply

Adore

You.

-Keymoni

Son

It is my womb that formed you.

I carried you with purpose

and gave birth to pain.

Cursed you with our ancestors' eyes

Their blood flows through your veins.

So you were doomed from the beginning.

Targets since birth

You've inherited your fathers' genes

His features

and his skin.

They will resent you.

They'll view you as a weapon instead of a blessing.

A curse instead of a compliment.

They'll destroy you.

But only if you let them.

Always remember

You are Royalty.

Coiled in Courage.

A King.

Formed from my womb.

-Keith

Overnight

I was wholesome once,

But he stripped me of my innocence overnight.

He would wait until the lights were out

When no one was watching.

His fingers would creep up into my cocooned sheets and muscle its way into my purity.

My eyes clenched shut

Muffled under his hand as he covered my lips.

No one could hear my cries.

I could do nothing.

I lied in my bed waiting for someone to save me

Waiting for my salty tears to dry

Waiting for him to finish.

I had spoken once before of your grotesque fetish,

But my mother chose to dwell in denial and try to convince me that my atrocity was only a figment of my imagination.

She said, "We reside in a society that says hush that things like this does not happen in black families and will not be discussed."

So I went back to my bed

Dreading the nights to come.

Waiting for someone to save me

Waiting for my salty tears to dry

Waiting for someone to listened

Waiting for him to finish.

S.W.A.K

Where's the instruction booklet for forgiving yourself?
I need the blueprint.
A step-by-step guide, so that I can stop blaming myself for what you did.

> At 7 years old
> He took it
> Upon himself
> To use his
> fingers to
> open my unsealed
> envelope
> and read the poems inside of me...
> without my consent.
>
> 'Til this day
> I still condemn myself
> for your lack of self control.
>
> Did I have it coming?
> was my smile
> to bright?
> Was I
> asking for it?
> Was my
> clothes to tight?
>
> Who is responsible for you violating me?
> Do I blame my absent father?
> Or
> Should I blame
> my mother
> for not protecting me
> from the hunter
> who saw me
> as his prey.
> This mail man
> who hand delivered
> My future
> insecurities,
> depression,
> and paranoia.
> I wish
> that I could
> return to sender
> this
> post traumatic stress,
> Forgive myself,
> Close this envelope
> Filled with poems.
> And **S**eal it **W**ith **A** **K**iss.

PREY

The world will try to shut your mouth and silence you

If you choose to speak the truth.

They will blame you for playing victim

and make excuses for the predator.

She lied about her age

She's Fast

She wanted it

She dresses too sexy

Her shape

Her curves

Her smile

Says different.

The pedophile

Preys on

Our

Babies with bodies

Just vulnerable victims

Naive and ignorant.

Easily convinced

And Brainwashed.

He is the pied piper

Who lures

Our girls

and kills them

Metaphorically,

Mentally,

Emotionally.

and yet the world will try

To silence YOU.

Abortion

Like a honeybee

in search for nectar
you transferred pollen

and impregnated me,
then left me for a titan arum.
In the garden I grew
in between my legs
what produced
where two buds
that grew into
gorgeous magnolias
I developed other flowers,
Roses and Orchids
but I did not allow
them to flourish.
The terror of tending
overwhelmed you
so they
were murdered
by fear.
The afterbirth
was poetry.

Garden

I have plucked pieces of me from the earth and handed it to you.

What was once admired for its beauty

has gone and withered away.

When I trusted you to water it.

and now

all I have left

are perished petals

and suffocated stems

where only weeds grow.

My garden is wiltered green

and I have grown weary

of letting you plant seeds in me

with ill intentions.

My harvest can't manifest with rotten soil

and I cannot reap with your rancid soul.

My purpose was not

only to be plucked and put on pedestals

or wrapped with intricate bows

for admiration and not appreciation.

The intention was to

Evolve and Grow

into something divine.

I've realized

You

Didn't know

The first thing about gardening.

Cactus

When you made your exit

Out of my life
With no explanation

or reason

it didn't faze me at all.

I was already familiar

with that detrimental feeling

of abandonment

and rejection.

My heart could bear

the coldest conditions.

Just like a cactus

I learned to adapt.

My father

had taught me

long ago

the valuable lesson

that everything you lose

Isn't a loss.

Sometimes you have to lose

to win

and sometimes you have to

Let go

To gain.

His negligence served as a seed to help me grow

without water,

without air,

without light.

And even in darkness....

I *STILL* flowered.

                                                               Just like a cactus.

Once Upon a Time

Pardon me for not believing in fairy tale endings.

It all one big delusional daydream

in the land of love and make believe surrounded by a sea of lies and deceit.

I do not Frolic in fantasies

or meditate in myths.

The thought of playing a fool

and falling in love again

makes me sick to my stomach

like when Snow White ate the poison apple and fainted.

We tell our daughters these whimsical stories

but we forget to finish

leaving them naive to the risk of losing.

 We fail to confess

how at the end of the story

The Princess suffers.

In my world

Tiana was bamboozled

Ariel was exiled

Jasmine was cheated

Belle was abused

Pocahontas was depressed

Mulan was lost

Rapunzel cried when

Sleeping Beauty died

and Cinderella broke her glass slipper

And filed for divorce.

There is no happily ever after

No prince charming

or true loves kiss.

Just fiction and fantasy.

Truth is, fairytales can transform into nightmares.

So if you ever find yourself trapped in a castle

Don't become the damsel in distress

waiting for a knight in shining armor to come save you

Be your own hero.

Half

I looked at the glass half-full only to find out that you were looking at it half empty.

How could I be so naive to entertain your capability of loving me the way that I loved you?

I loved you with all of me only to be half-loved by you.

Why did I indulge in such heartache?

Why would I live a half-life of loving you when losing you would cause me a whole death?

I could not mask my feelings for you.

Maybe I expressed my feelings for you too bluntly

I should have kept silent.

Maybe then, I would not be affected by the impact of your rejection.

You accepted my love for you so loudly only to offer your love in silence

Quiet.

I fantasized that you could love me whole-ly

Only to be left empty

You had given me false hopes, dampened dreams and vacant promises.

I was hungry for you,

Ready to devour a full course meal, but you only granted an appetizer

not enough to satiate my hunger

Ready to take a full gulp, but you only offered a sip

not enough to quench my thirst.

What made you unable to love me?

You were a whole being capable of loving whole-heartedly but sat at the table half-hearted.

I wanted all of you, but you were incapable of meeting me half-way and that led us nowhere but…

Back at the table

Looking at the glass

Half empty

Intoxicated

From the moment I took my first sip, I drowned.
It hit me unexpectedly, and as the alcohol rushed through my bloodstream
I started losing myself.
They say don't drink and drive, but I took the fast lane.
I was unaware that my destination would be a dead end.
Dysfunctional.
I had one too many drinks.
At first, the buzz felt so good
but after the seventh one, I got out of my character.
Things became a blur, fuzzy, shady.
A cloud of despair,
and soon after the alcohol irritated my stomach
made me throw up, sick, and nauseated.
I consumed so much, and instead of drowning my sorrows away
I felt dehydrated;
I didn't receive the effect I had expected.
This alcohol was disastrous
It aged me
Stressed me out beyond imagination.
I wasn't myself.
I had been poisoned.
My lungs were damaged
Heart broken
Liver destroyed
The alcohol I seeked as an escape imprisoned me.
I was suffering
But I kept on consuming one drink after the other
Doing the same thing over and over
Expecting a different outcome
I was insane, Delusional even.
I started to hallucinate,
Seeing things
I wanted to see
Making excuses
Not accepting the fact that I had became
ADDICTED.
My symptoms were clear
Anxiety, tremors, palpitations and sweating.
My phobia
Was being alone,
Isolated
I was dependent on alcohol and that very substance would cause the death of me
I was intoxicated...
And as I woke up the next morning with a headache and hangover.
I looked over
At the bottle next to me.
The substance I had consumed was YOU.
And the bottle simply read...

Drowning

I dove deep into an ocean of love

hoping

that even though

I couldn't swim

you wouldn't let me drown.

Already

in too deep

I struggled

to reach the surface

and catch my breath.

Gasping for air,

I reach out my arm

in expectation that

you would grab my hand

and pull me up.

Trying to get a hold of something

that was not there,

I sank deeper

and died slowly.

I wished that you would put on your life jacket and

dive in to rescue me.

Instead,

you stood there

                                                and watch me drown

Catch

With bait on hook
he caught me.
Mouth pierced
lip split
he held me above water
while he contemplated if
I was a trophy worth keeping.
Gasping for dear life
battered and blood-stained
I looked into his eyes
and begged for mercy because
I could not live without water
so I fought a good fight
with all my might
to be released from this
thin line of wire
the only thing
holding me back
from being where I belonged.
The moment
he took his eyes off me
I took
the the leap of faith
that meant life or death for me.
I broke the line
and swam against the current
with a piece of that wire
still with me
as he looked on and realized
although there are plenty of fishes in the sea
I will forever be

                                                        The one that got away.

Sugar

He would ask me how long it was going to take me to come home

because he couldn't bear being away from me for too long.
He would text me sweet nothings
in the middle of the day
and tell me how much I meant to him.

Bring me flowers for no reason
bearing wrapped gifts
of chocolate covered strawberries.
Write sweet letters
and dedicate romantic love songs to me.
Little did I know
that the showering of affection
was him hiding his guilt.
It was calculated mischief
Disguised as a caring heart.
What I thought was sweet as sugar
was camouflaging salt.

Walls

The walls wanted to talk to me

and voice all the things unseen.

They wanted to speak of the spines you had against them.

Tell me about those silent footsteps you had walking into the foundation

we had built.

Whisper the names of the women you

had lay their head against my pillow.

The jezebels you would have in my place,

while I was gone.

The walls had eyes

they could see what I was blind to.

If only these walls could talk.

Insomniac

I am tired of these sleepless nights.

I am waiting for them to transform into unexpected breakthroughs

Your memory seems to sneak up on me at night

and my tired eyes are frustrated.

Like a thief in the night,

You take my peace away from me.

When I am most vulnerable

Most lonely.

I am tired of your memories

Deliberant disobeyence

To my tranquility.

You have taken a toll

On my eyes.

My body

and my heart.

I am exhausted.

I am worn down by you.

Even in a world full of second chances

there isn't enough room for your sorry's and I love you's

to refresh me from my tiredness;

and how fed up I am of hearing your bullshit.

I am, tired of forgiving.

I am tired of losing sleep

I am tired of

being sick and tired.

Performance

You tried to create a love story with-in a tragedy

With well-rehearsed scripted lines

and fitted costumes

but your performance left me skeptical.

I could see right through you

Like the lens of a camera.

I was the director and you were the actor

Masquerading as my soul mate.

You could be nominated for an academy award.

You were so good at pretending

Always acting on cue.

With Simulated smiles.

Counterfeit caresses.

and fabricated laughter

Locked in an image of

Loyalty, sincerity, and honor.

I got so used to it

That I grew attached to the mask.

The fantasy you fed me was impressive but fake.

The reality was realizing that I only loved you for

Who you pretended to be,

A Well-orchestrated faithful husband.

So take a bow

And prepare

For round of applause and standing ovations

You gave a grand performance.

FIN.

Pretend

I pretended to make sense of it all

by nodding my head in reassurance

but I could not gather my thoughts

around your excuses.

Why?

How could you do this?

I couldn't comprehend how someone I love

could betray me.

So I closed my eyes and pretended

not to feel.

I pretended that my unhappiness didn't exist

I pretended not to see the warnings signs

the erased text messages

or the late nights at the studio

I was unwilling to see the red flags

because I was in love.

So I closed my eyes and pretended that you cared,

pretended that you loved me back.

I ignored that chill feeling

when our souls had disconnected

because it wasn't supposed to be like this;

but our flames had perished,

It diminished without me even noticing

that,

You cheated me

and still

I closed my eyes and pretended It never happened.

Carpenter

I tried to build a broken man

Cut deep into my flesh

and Carve pieces of me to make him whole

His secretary

His lover

His backbone

His rider

His everything

I built a man

With all my bricks

and filled

all his nooks and crannies

With fragments of my heart.

and when I grew weak

With nothing left

No plaster

No blocks

No wood or glue

I realized

I gave so much of me

 to you

I had nothing

 for myself.

Bag Man

(An Ode to Erykah Badu)

Bag lady you gon' hurt your back, dragging all them bags like that
 I guess nobody ever told you
that all you need to hold on to is you,
and that when a man truly loves a woman he'll do whatever he has to do
See, the definition of a bag man
 is a man who is unable to carry his own weight
 so he will use the manipulation of his words and his dick
 to convince you to stay.
Have you carry all of his burdens
and his emotional pain,
Put them on your shoulders for his personal gain.
Bag lady you gon' miss your bus
You can't hurry up
'Cause you got too much stuff
And he refuses to step up.
No job, No Car, and nowhere to lay his head
So he leeches off you,
With his hand out
ready to beg.
Depends on you to solves his problems
All his baby mamma drama
He can't keep up with his child support
So you pay all his debt.
He takes so much from you
That you ain't got nothing left

See, that weight you try so hard to carry
because he can't hold his own.
Will build his ego up
 and only weight you down.
So Lady,
 Let go of that sack
 on your back
It's time for you
 to unpack.
I know it's hard sometimes but you got to learn to move on.
Tell that scrub to catch a cab
Better yet,
Call Tyrone.

Slave
I have spent years next to you every night
knowing you were incapable of loving me
the way I deserved to be loved.

I have given you parts of me
that I knew belonged to someone else,
because God never intended for me to fall for you.

Time and time again

 I have made excuses
 and have tried to make us work.

Children,
Years invested
Conventional
Routine

So I stayed in this cage
 and I continued going back to my habit
just like an addict and her addiction.

Within that...
I have lost myself with you
My faith
My confidence
My self-worth
and self-esteem

Day after day
 I keep accepting this emotional and mental abuse
and it has taken its toll on me.

 All of the lies
 All of the cheating.

It has been so long since I have felt free.
 So long that
Happiness has become foreign to me.

And every time I get the courage to leave
 Just like a boomerang I end up coming right back
because I have deceived myself into believing

That this time it'll be better
This time he will change
This time he will love me enough
 not to hurt me again.

I never realized
that I was in marital bondage.

My heart was enslaved
by a master of manipulation
and every time I would try and escape
he would inflict more and more pain.

Massa was on his high horse,
Whip in hand
ready to put those slashes of
betrayal on my back.

and I longed
for the day
I get the courage to
cut the chains
and runaway.

Declared Free
January 22, 2018
11:00 A.M

Vows

I vowed that I would take you

to be my lawfully wedded husband to have and to hold,

from that day forward

for better

for worse

for richer

for poorer

in sickness and in health

until death do us part

Our rings symbolized

how we promised

to be committed

to each other
and then we

sealed it with a kiss.
A decade later
At my darkest
In my struggles
Unwell
Unhappy
And at my wits end
You showed me that

those vows were said

with fingers crossed
behind your back

YOU were to unlawful to be my wedded husband.

September 27, 2013 (The Day we wed)

September 13, 2015 (The Day I Left)

Curse

When I was a child
My Grandfather left his family
and started a new one with another woman.

When I became a teen
I witness my mother
go through a dreadful divorce.

When I became a woman

I wanted to break the cycle.

I fell in love

and had a beautiful family.

I wanted to disown the plague

 that haunted our family lineage.

Renounce the inheritance
 of broken homes
Passed down to me
from generation to generation.

Today, I have failed.

I pray that I do not

pass down this curse

to my daughter.

Hungry

I was willing to starve

For the sake of you and me.

But you didn't love me enough.

I was willing to sacrifice it all.

But you took the source

that was feeding you for granted,

Only to seek

Momentary satisfaction

and entertain the distraction

That would kill US.

How could you stomach that?

fathom the thought of losing everything

We've always wanted.

Family and Foundation

Love and Loyalty

for temporary cravings.

Compromising home cooked meals

for microwave dinners.

Left empty.

What were you hungry for?

You allowed your vices to dictate your decisions.

Your appetite desired

Something sweet, but left you salty.

A Stomach full of nothing.

Next time be selective.

Next time

Acquire a taste for something everlasting.

Conflict

I hated you

But my flesh would rise against me and disagree.

Even when I couldn't bear the thought of you

I would welcome you with opens arms

and let you in.

Like a worm burrowing into healthy flesh.

My flesh would take the lead and ignore what my mind was telling me.

How stubborn she could be

To know that you were no good

But still itch for your companionship.

Like cocaine to an addict

This temporary high surpassed the pain you supplied.

My heart and my mind said no

But my body

Would always say yes.

I wish that they all would bury the hatchet

and grasp

That the heart makes better decisions

because the flesh is weak.

My flesh would point us to what seem to be so tantalizing

Only for my heart to feel its bitterness.

My flesh refused to follow directions

Until one day

It led us to the realization

That I didn't hate you.

I hated who I was

for loving you.

Robbery

All I ever dreamed of
Was A Happy Ever After.
That is the life I wanted.
I deserved that life,
but you robbed me.

You robbed me of my time
My dreams
and my emotions.
Dressed in all black
With a ski mask covering your face

You took the chance I had of showing my daughter what love looks like.
To show my son
How a man that genuinely loves the woman who carries his seed
Is treated
The mother of your child
For years
You held my heart hostage
Armed with lies
Weapon in hand
You took your pistol
And aimed at my chest
After you got what you wanted
You pulled the trigger.
and emptied the clip

                                                                                              POW!

Band- Aid

My wounds were fresh.
and instead of letting time
heal my heart
I kept covering the hurt
you inflicted upon me
with a band aid.
I hid my pain
while you poured salt on my flesh
and kept it burning.
You were the worst kind of man
you listened to all my pain,
my past,
my struggles
and put it upon yourself
to watch me hurt again.
When I thought that
I had healed
you kept picking at the scabs
and reopening the lacerations.
Until the anguish became unbearable.
The sting from the band aid would have to
subdue
I could no longer
ignore the infection
that was growing internally.
You caused more harm
then you could cover.
There was no need for a Band aid
anymore
When I needed surgery.

Band aids were for cuts.
I needed stitches.
I needed air.
I needed healing.

Death

I went to a funeral yesterday
and said my final goodbyes.
It was my duty to give the eulogy.
So I walked up to the alter and
Stood over your breathless corpse
 Unbothered.
 Undisturbed by your death because you once tried to kill me
and this was my chance at freedom,
My opportunity for a new birth.
So I stood there
Head held high
With no tears shed.
And said
"Here lies pain.
I suffered long enough
With Stab wounds to the heart
Broken Promises
and Shots of betrayal.
Drowned by years of Disloyalty
Abortions
and Adultery.
Your death was inevitable.
and it was my time to let go.
Because although you were my lifeline
I was nothing
To you
So I prepared for your demise
and had already planned your funeral
Picked a plot
and insurance
 So I would be just fine."
With dirt in my hands
Over your casket
 I said this with no remorse
"This is my final farewell
May you rest in hell
Ashes to Ashes
Dust to Dust
Death to you and this poisoned relationship. "

                                                            Wiped my hands
                                                            Walked away
                                                     and never looked back.

Senses

The memory of me
has not died.
It resides
in the back
of your mind
and triggers
with everything
in sight.
My laugh
an echo
in your ear,
My smile
a dwelling
in your thoughts,
My touch
an impression
in your heart.
These lips
still linger in your palate.
The sweet aroma
of my body
has not worn off
even when you
pretend to forget;
I know I haunt your dreams.
I *ain't* sorry
for having your soul
hidden
in my back pocket.

Recipe to Recovery

I took the pain I felt in all at once

All of the bad and the betrayal.

Let it set in deep inside of me.

I cried all the tears

until my eyes went dry.

Listen to all the break up songs

and pacified the pain with poetry

In hopes of getting over you.

I cut my hair

and burned our pictures

I exercised,

Detoxed

and deleted you

out of my life.

I looked myself

in the mirror

and saw me for who I Am.

Just like I saw him for who he was.

No more blindness

No more pain

No more clinging to that toxic love.

I let the pain I felt change me

I saw him take those steps

to walk out of our home.

and built the strength to move forward,

Leave

and

Move on.

Karma

I have been waiting,
waiting for karma
to *attack* your life
like the bitch she really is
Threaten you with a bark of aggression

Stare and *Show* her teeth
Growl And *Lunge* at you.
But it seems,
 that karma is all *bark* and no *bite*
because she has been *playing dead*
 otherwise
 she has *rolled over* on me
since my life
 has been *spinning* out of control
and I for the life of me
 cannot *fetch*
 why it seems like
no harm has come to you and you are moving on
While my life is *standing still*
 and I am the only one suffering.
Karma and time
must be *shaking hands*
Because I have been waiting…
Waiting for time to heal these wounds
but it seems that both Karma and time is working
at their own pace…Oh how

Karma IS SUCH A *BITCH!*

Rx

(Rebound)

I'm sorry,

I've been hurt.

So pardon me for using you as medicine for my ailment.

Your conversation was a remedy

To get my mind off what was killing me

Internally.

I needed you

for the moment.

So I swallowed you whole like a pill

and took advantage of what you had to offer

Your kisses were an antibiotic

and the sex was my antidote.

A sedative for my chaos.

I laid naked next to you,

 But

It wasn't you that I wanted.

You were just a temporary fix for the damage he did.

A way for me to release this toxic serum

He injected in me.

A self-prescribed convenient cure

 for my suffering

My heart was infected

You were my healing.

My prescription.

Bending Blues

I have lost myself before,
I drank
until I felt numb
I took pills
with hopes of overdosing
I drowned
 in a bathtub full of my own tears
I drew a gun
against my temple
with the desire that this despair would diminish.
I know what depression feels like
It suffocates
It consumes
It crawls on your skin
and bites your soul
with its poisonous venom
It seeps its fangs deep inside your pores
It voyages through your veins
It tightens like a noose around your neck
It weighs on your shoulders
and feels like you're carrying the world.
It is heavy.
It hits your soul
Like bullets hits black
leaving wounds behind.
I have been there
and sometimes I don't know

Whether

I'm leaving or going

Breathing or drowning

or dying

I have lost myself to darkness
So close to the edge
I can feel myself falling
down a cliff of bottomless pain

I fail
I cry
I bend
But I never seem to break.

Incompetence

Despite the well applied make up

Long lashes,

Gray contacts,

Three packs of Brazilian.

The implants,

The MCM bag,

The designer clothes and shoes

and the accessories from the boutique;

She is UNHAPPY.

It's written all over her face.

She must have

 low self esteem

accepting a man that cheats on her,

Beats on her

and abuses her verbally.

What a disgrace.

Her insecurities are on display

but she tries so hard to hide them

Behind the Cartier glasses

Is a black eye.

The night before she was slapped up

with Gucci flip-flops

Left bruised up.

Ego fucked up.

Later to hear

"I'm sorry, it won't happen again

So here's my card

Go cop the New Giuseppe's

and forget how I use you

Manipulate and abuse you."

BRAIN WASHED

She defines happiness with

Materialistic

Partying in V.I.P and taking trips.

She brags to her friends about

 how much he loves me

Accepts a ring with

No commitment.

Crying for attention.

She doesn't realize she was a pawn in his chess game.

Used to make moves, get A. D's, and steal identities.

But does not have an identity of her own.

I wished that her self-esteem was as high as those 6-inch heels

As rich as her appearance

and as full as her injected booty.

Since there was no value in her beauty

Because she was full of fraudulence.

A slave to her own whims, he was her master.

He possessed the ability to calculate correctly

Her destruction.

She lacked

 Self- confidence

Incompetent of

Self- love

Acceptance

I look into the mirror

and nick pick everything I see that is wrong with me.

From the color of my eyes

To the acne on my skin.

To the shape of my nose

and the gap in between my teeth.

These things don't typically appeal to what

Society think is beautiful.

So I cover what God created as a masterpiece

With contacts and MAC make-up

Wishing I could make up

What he messed up

But God does not make any mistakes.

We implement self-hate

When we put society's views of beauty on a pedestal

and idolized these celebrities with

Big breast, Small waist

Fat asses, Yet…BAD TASTE.

When we realize that, no one is perfect

and   not everything can be pretty on its surface;

That beauty is not just skin,

because true beauty comes from within.

We won't crave society's views of perfection.

Since every imperfection is a blessing

and true beauty comes from _acceptance_.

Reborn

I have been so many things
Broken
Mistreated
Torn
Rejected
Lost
Used
Empty
Numb
Lonely
and Scared
and Through it all a part of me dies
with each encounter.
But because I have embrace the experience
I have witness my test become my testimony
and my pieces become my peace.
I had to decipher how to
wash away the past

replenish in the present

 prepare for the future

 and delete the fear within me

I am now
Healed
Whole
Confident
Satisfied
Mended
and loved
I had to acknowledge that in death,
There is always an opportunity for _rebirth_.

Naked

He said

when I stripped down my walls

and all the barriers I built

leaving myself bare and vulnerable

No Foundation

No cover girl

No concealer

to cover my blemishes

No M.A.C to cover my scars

I was the most beautiful.

Undressed and undisguised

Unguarded and unafraid

to expose

my true beauty.

Just raw and defenseless.

You told me that my art

could never exist

without my bare beauty

being displayed

to the visible eyes

You showed me that

beauty is in the eye of the beholder

because you loved me

past my flaws

and all my imperfections.

Woman

Being a black woman
is complex.
Both joy and ecstasy
But relentless and unending.
They want us to
Be strong and soft
Tender and tough
Be light not Dark
Polished.
There is no room for error
Stress
Depression
Anger
Anxiety
Loss or Grief
We are not supposed to feel
We are supposed to
Endure
Entertain
Enlighten
Evoke
Enchant
We are only to be enjoyed
Don't hurt
Don't cry
Don't scream
Be Silent
Don't Speak
We are supposed to
Be submissive
Listen
Nourish
Nurture
Build
Survive in war.
These are the expectations for being…..*black girl*
Mesmerizing
Ambitious
Gifted
Innovative
Courageous

Homemade

Remarkably moist. Intensely chocolate-y. A tried and true gem that has been beloved for generations. Serve it and see why.

Pre-Heat the oven to 350°F.

Gather all ingredients

Grab two bowls

In one stir together

Milk and honey

In the other sift

Cinnamon, brown sugar, cocoa and gold dust.

Combine the two

and beat all elements with an electric mixer until blended

Light yet firm

Gradually mix in

Strength, ambition, creativity and faith.

Sprinkle fearlessness

Add a dash of sassiness

and don't forget the blood, sweat, and tears

Pour into 2 parchment-lined 9-inch round pans made with melanin

Bake until a toothpick inserted in centers comes out clean.

Remove& cool completely.

Meanwhile, microwave caramel and butter in large bowl until melted, stirring every second trials and tribulations.

Use to fill in layers.

Decorate with frosting of laughter and smiles or other sweetened fillings

Gaze at its greatness

Cut into her soft seductive texture.

Take a bite

and taste her orgasmic flavor.

The cake is irresistible, so

Serve others carefully this is ...

                                                                     Homemade Black Woman
                                                                          (Made from scratch)

Sweet Tea

I've found myself thirsty.

Yearning for an organic beverage

To satisfy my dehydration.

No sugar added.

A natural sweetener.

Dark like melanin

Raw as molasses and

Sweet like nectar.

Hot and healing

Calming and charming

Securing and southern

and comforting.

Mouthwatering and mesmerizing.

I found myself

 thirsty for you.

So I drank, swallowed

and delighted in the deliciousness

of your steamy cup of

tempting tea,

Birthing flavor

to my taste buds

                                                          (Aaaaaaah)

Custom Made

He saw what you had done
and used his hands to fix it.
He didn't know how it was broken
or what went wrong;
but knew he was chosen to repair
what you ruined.
He never witnessed the pain
just picked up the pieces
that were left hanging
by a string
with hardly a thread to pull.
He stitch the seams
that was one tug away
from falling apart.
Patch by patch
linen from wool
with the needle and thread
of faith and prayer.
The epiphany
was knowing
 that her fabric
was cut from a different cloth
and that
 their love
would be
custom made.

Artist

I laid back on white silk sheets
Legs spread like an easel
Waiting for you to create art.
Your tongue was the paint brush
Dipping into pigment
Dragging its bristles
Onto my blank canvas.
I was naked,
Yearning to burst
Eyes rolled back
Into a kaleidoscope
of vibrant colors
 As I grip your dome
and you expressed paint
In every stroke.
My legs began to tremble
As you beg me to peak
and stain our sheets.
Beads of sweat smeared and dripping
Decorating our bodies as
 I run away
and you chase the frost
In between my velvet walls.
You use your labored fingers to
Fondle me
Coloring my clitoris.
Your brush left glossy
Coated in cream.
Lips dressed in ivory sheets
Tinted in whitewash
Soaked with my ART?
The painting was inside me
 You titled it
Heavens Residue

Live

Death is inevitable

but first we must live.

Live and love.

Love wild and free

Love like you mean it.

Love With every fiber of your being

from your skin to your marrow

Love wholeheartedly

Love unapologetically

with no regrets.

Love like you've never been broken

Love with patience

Love with kindness

Love selflessly

Love truthfully

Love hopelessly

Love respectively

In a world full of chaos

There are 3 things for certain

It is life, love, and death.

and the greatest of these is love.

Cherish it.

Live it.

Mona Lisa

The true story behind her smile

left room for speculation

you couldn't distinguish

whether she was

happy

disappointed

or in love.

she wasn't a perfect portrait

and there was nothing special about her canvas

but you could not deny that she was truly a work of art.

what made her so different?

Even in a museum full of art

scholars would study her,

 artist would make music romantizing about her,

and people would travel around the world just to take a glimpse.

I came to the conclusion that we were just the same

that just like her

God handled me so delicately.

little by little.

piece by piece.

he designed all the qualities that I possessed

that I could be nothing less than alluring.

just like Davinci created a work of art when he painted the Mona Lisa

God created a masterpiece

when he made one version of me.

I AM MONA.

Ayiti (Haiti)

My ancestors blood

has stained the land.

We have fought through pain and tears

with all our might and prayers.

With nothing but hope and courage.

They televise our sorrows

but never our strengths.

They forget to mention how

we liberated from

Slavery

How we survived our struggles

in every disaster

From Diasporas to oppression

from hurricanes to earthquakes

My Island

A country of multi ethnicity and color

The First

Black

Republic

Of the world.

You've made history

and

I am proud

that your plasma runs through my veins.

Ayiti you are Revolutionary.

Ayiti (Creole Version)

Zansèt san mwen

Èske gen tach peyi a.

Nou te goumen nan doulè ak dlo nan je

Ak tout pouvwa nou yo ak lapriyè.

Avèk anyen men espwa ak kouraj.

Yo televize lapenn nou

Men se pa fòs nou.

Yo bliye mansyone jan

Nou te libere nan

Esklavaj

Ki jan nou te siviv lit nou yo

Nan tout dezas

Soti nan dyaspora opresyon

Soti nan siklòn tranblemanntè

Zile mwen

Yon peyi nan milti etnisite ak koulè

Premye a

Nwa

Repiblik

Nan mond lan.

Ou te fè istwa

Ak

Mwen fyè

Ki plasma ou kouri atravè venn mwen an.

Ayiti ou se Revolisyonè.

Survival

I have been...
Beat before,
so the impact between
belt and skin does not scare me.

Broken before,
so pieces of me
in poetry
flow freely

Burnt,
Like a woman scorned.
so fire simply
ignites my fury

I have been
Betrayed;
so the knife
piercing through my backs flesh
does not hurt
as much.

I have gotten so used to
looking at circles
of **black** and **blue**
and marks from wounds
as **badges** of survival.

I wear
Bruises like **medallions**
I wear
Heartache like **trophies**
I wear
Scars like **crowns**

Poetry

You are perfection

you are my first,

my last,

my infinite.

With every letter

every word

every sentence

and every stanza

you exemplify who I am.

You are my confidant, my best friend

and the love of my life.

I pour my heart out to you

because you speak when I am voiceless.

You carry the weight of my words

and exude every emotion

that I attempt to hide.

I spill my souls ink on paper,

In hopes that the bleak will be beautiful.

I am dripping poetry.

You

are my canvas.

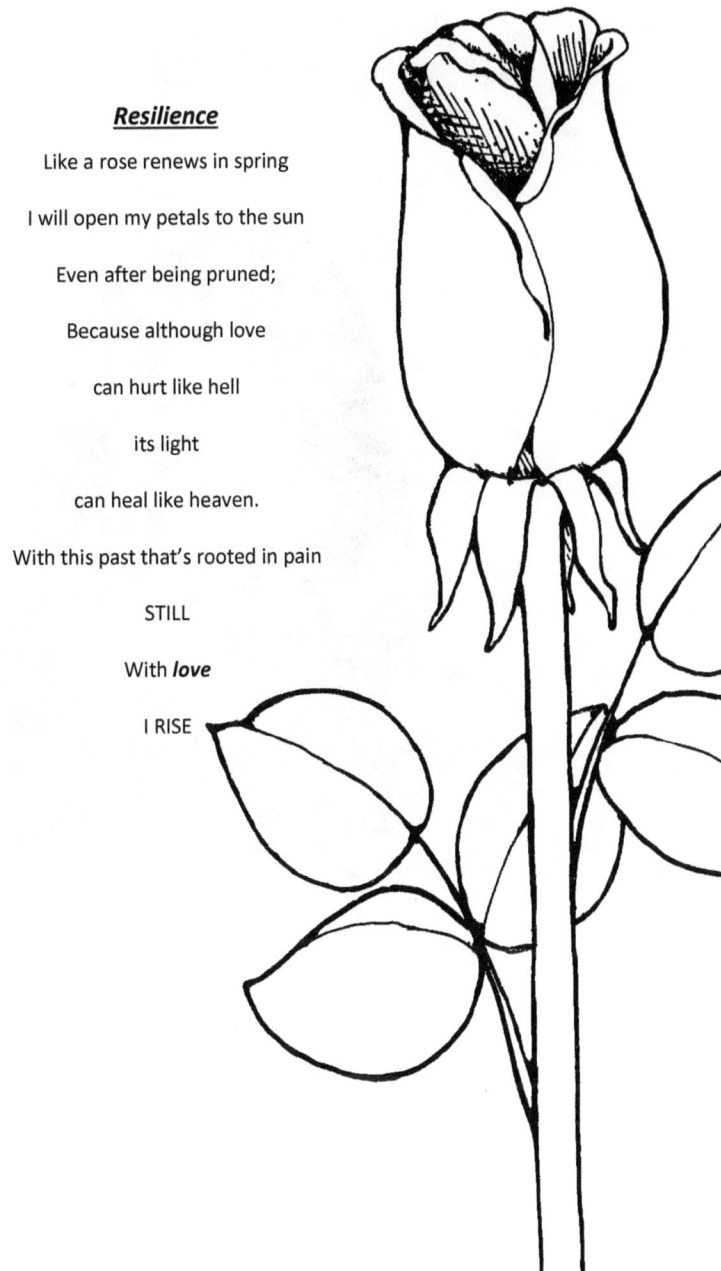

Resilience

Like a rose renews in spring

I will open my petals to the sun

Even after being pruned;

Because although love

can hurt like hell

its light

can heal like heaven.

With this past that's rooted in pain

STILL

With *love*

I RISE

I have finally made peace with my truths
and have transformed my pieces into a masterpiece. -Monica

A Word from Mona

I used to be afraid to tell people what I was going through or what I am going through because of the fear of being weak and judged. For so long, I painted a pretty picture of love and happiness but internally I was broken. I walked on eggshells afraid that someone would perceive me as being weak. Mona's Masterpiece Fifty Pieces of Poetry is about taking my weakness and transforming it into strength. Creating art with my writing, being transparent, baring it all and being naked with vulnerability. I had to learn that my vulnerability was the source of my healing, that my tears told truths, and that my pain had purpose. Without the pain, I would not be able to articulate my words and use the pen as a tool for my therapy.
I decided to put my pain on paper. In this book I shed my skin and share my soul with you. I hope that my words inspire others to express what is in their heart and to create their own art; their own masterpiece.

To The Reader

I send my deepest gratitude, my love and blessings to all of the people who support me and saw greater in me when I did not see it within myself. You all served as pieces in pushing me to complete my masterpiece.
You are holding a piece of me in your hands. This book exemplifies who I am; it holds pieces of my pain and my faith. These words were painfully written and shall be beautifully read.
May my words rise and my art, my legacy, reign forever.

About the book

Mona's Masterpiece Fifty Pieces of Poetry is a compilation of poems about life, love, lessons and self evolution. She titled her book Mona's Masterpiece because her poetry consists of pieces of the moments she battled with in her life; she tackles subjects like family, molestation, love, relationships, heartbreak and self-acceptance to name a few. Mona's raw and often-relatable poetry transports readers through a journey of various pieces of her life. Unravel her words and discover the essence of who Mona truly is.

Inspirations

While writing this book I listened to some of my favorite artist, music from Tupac Amaru Shakur, Erykah Badu, Beyonce' Knowles, Fantasia Barrino, Aretha Franklin and recordings of my favorite poet Maya Angelou inspired some of my pieces.

About the Writer

Monica Alfred also known as Mona is a woman first, a mother, a daughter, a sister, and a writer.

Born and raised in the heart of Miami Florida on September 6. Her passion for writing began at the tender age of seven when she started writing in journals to relieve from the pain she felt at home.

A survivor of sexual abuse, heartbreak and divorce she expresses her deepest inner demons in order to heal from her hurt and heartache. When she is not writing she enjoys listening to rhythm and blues, watching movies, spending time and creating intimate memories with her children Keymoni and Keith. Mona's Masterpiece Fifty Pieces of Poetry is her debut collection of writing with plans to write a novel in connection with her poetry.

She hopes that the world sees a piece of her in Mona's Masterpiece.

www.ingramcontent.com/pod-product-compliance
Lightning Source LLC
Chambersburg PA
CBHW070921180426
43192CB00038B/2149